EDGE
BOOKS

SUPER TRIVIA COLLECTION

THIS BOOK IS TOP SECRET

BY CHERYL BLACKFORD

A COLLECTION OF AWESOME MILITARY TRIVIA

CAPSTONE PRESS
a capstone imprint

Edge Books are published by Capstone Press,
1710 Roe Crest Drive, North Mankato, Minnesota 56003.
www.capstonepub.com

Library of Congress Cataloging-in-Publication Data
Blackford, Cheryl.
This book is top secret : a collection of awesome military trivia / by Cheryl Blackford.
p. cm.—(Edge books. Super trivia collection)
Includes bibliographical references and index.
Summary: "Describes a variety of military facts, including vehicles, weapons, troops, and past
battles"—Provided by publisher.
Audience: Ages 8-12.
ISBN 978-1-4296-8591-7 (library binding)
ISBN 978-1-62065-233-6 (ebook PDF)
1. United States. Armed Forces—Juvenile literature. 2. Military weapons—Juvenile literature.
I. Title. II. Title: Awesome military trivia.
A23.B538 2013
355.00973—dc23   2011049864

Editorial Credits

Erika L. Shores, editor; Tracy McCabe, designer; Wanda Winch, media researcher;
    Laura Manthe, production specialist

Photo Credits

AP Images: U.S. Navy, 15 (bottom); The Bridgeman Art Library International: © Look and Learn/Private
Collection/Ron Embleton, 26, Archives Charmet/Bibliotheque Nationale, Paris, France/French School,
27 (b); Corbis, 28 (top); Courtesy of AeroVironment, Inc., 25 (b); Courtesy of BAE Systems, 19 (t);
HULC ® photo courtesy of Lockheed Martin. Copyright 2012. All rights reserved, 22 (b); The Museum
of the Confederacy, 27 (t); NASA, 10 (b); National Archives & Records Administration (NARA), 28
(b), NARA: U.S. Army Sgt. Adrian C. Duff, 29 (t); National WASP WWII Museum, 10 (t); Newscom:
Album, 29 (b), Boston Dynamics/2009/WENN.com, cover (bm), 23 (b); Shutterstock: apdesign, cover
(grenade), 1, Dietmar Hoepfl, 13 (warthog), Doremi, 13 (tub), erwinwira11, 11 (bomb), Fernando Cortes,
(graffiti design), Lynx Aqua, 19 (b), Miguel Angel Salinas, 9 (t), mirabile, 24 (b), Steyno&Stitch, 7 (b); U.S.
Air Force Photo, 8 (b), 11 (t), 17 (t), U.S. Air Force Photo: Airman 1st Class Benjamin Wiseman, 13 (t),
Master Sgt. William Greer, cover (t), Master Sgt. Kevin J. Gruenwald, 16 (b), Roland Balik, 13 (b), Staff
Sgt. Lee O. Tucker, 4, 16 (t), Tech Sgt. James Pritchett, 12, Tech Sgt. Erik Gudmundson, 24 (t), TSGT
Ken Hammond, 20; U.S. Army Photo, 6, U.S. Army Photo: Jason Kaye, 18 (b), Sgt. Grant Matthes, 21
(b), Spec. Olanrewaju Akinwunmi, cover (br); U.S. Marine Corps, 21 (t), U.S. Marine Corps: Cpl. Brian
J. Slaght, 8 (t), Cpl. Jennifer J. Pirante, 23 (t), Lance Cpl. Joseph M. Peterson, 22 (t); U.S. Navy: Mass
Comm. Specialist 2nd Class Brian Morales, 15 (t), Mass Comm. Specialist 2nd Class John P. Curtis, 9 (b),
Mass Comm. Specialist 2nd Class Joshua T. Rodriguez, 25 (t), Mass Comm. Specialist 2nd Class Kyle
D. Gahlau, 7 (t), Mass Comm. Specialist 3rd Class Scott Pittman, 5 (t), 18 (t), Mass Comm. Specialist
3rd Class Shonna L. Cunningham, 14 (t), Mass Comm. Specialist Seaman Chad R. Erdmann, 17 (b),
Photographer's Mate 1st Class Ted Banks, 19 (m), Photographers' Mate 2nd Class Katrina Beeler, 11 (b),
Photographer's Mate 3rd Class M. Jeremie Yoder, 14 (b); U.S. Navy SEAL and SWCC, 5 (b)

Printed in the United States of America in Stevens Point, Wisconsin.
042013   007349R

TABLE OF CONTENTS

BEWARE THE PREDATOR

F-16 Fighting Falcon

What do falcons, ospreys, and seals have in common? If you said they're **predators**, you'd be right. And if you said they're all names of military aircraft or soldiers, you'd be right again. Dig into this book to uncover awesome facts about speedy F-16 Fighting Falcons, amazing V-22 Ospreys, and daring U.S. Navy SEALs. You'll also find out little-known facts about military battles of the past, the latest hi-tech military gear, and more.

predator—an animal that hunts other animals for food

V-22 Osprey

Chapter 1

FEARLESS FIGHTERS

They jump out of planes and swim underwater. They trudge through swampland and sweat in the desert heat. Who are they? They're the fearless fighters of the U.S. military.

The Special Forces are some of the toughest, best-trained military troops. Members of these top forces learn **unconventional warfare**. While regular soldiers only learn to use three or four weapons, Special Forces weapons sergeants are skilled at using 80. They can assemble and use anything from an old-fashioned slingshot to a modern machine gun.

U.S. Navy SEALs are fit and fearless. They have to be to finish the fourth week of BUD/S training. They spend this week running, swimming, crawling, or paddling boats. They slog through obstacle courses and carry logs and inflatable boats. They do all this and more with only four hours of sleep in five days.

SEALs have unusual ways of getting around. They use amphibious assault crafts and mini-submarines. SEALs and their inflatable rafts can be dropped into water from a helicopter. SEALs call this a "rubber duck" entry.

unconventional warfare—a way of fighting that is not like ordinary combat

inflatable—can be filled with air

amphibious—able to work on land and water

What do U.S. soldiers eat when they're in combat? It's called a Meal, Ready-to-Eat (MRE). A soldier drops a pouch of prepared food into a special heating bag and adds water. Minutes later a hot meal is ready. Now that's fast food!

In 1960 U.S. Air Force Captain Joseph W. Kittinger, Jr. made a record-breaking jump. He jumped from a balloon 20 miles (32 kilometers) above Earth to test out a new parachute system. Kittinger fell for nearly five minutes before his main parachute opened.

Sailors in the U.S. Navy speak their own language. They sleep in "racks" and shower in the "head." The wall is the "bulkhead" and the floor is the "deck." A "cranial" is a helmet and a "float coat" keeps them afloat if they fall overboard.

Cramming 6,000 crew members onto one ship doesn't leave much space for extra stuff. On Nimitz-class aircraft carriers, crew members sleep 60-to-a-room. Crew members have a storage bin under their bed and a locker the size of your school locker for their belongings.

They knew how to fly every kind of American military plane. But they were never allowed to fly them in combat. Women Airforce Service Pilots (WASP) trained male fighter pilots and flew other missions for the U.S. military during World War II (1939–1945). In 2010, nearly 66 years after the war, the WASP received Congressional gold medals for their service.

In 1995 U.S. Air Force Colonel Eileen Collins piloted a space shuttle. In 1999 she commanded the *Columbia* space shuttle. Colonel Collins is the first woman to pilot and command a space shuttle.

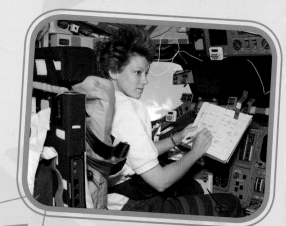

Today American military women do fly combat missions. Colonel Martha McSally was the first female Air Force pilot. In 1995 she became the first woman to fly a fighter jet in combat. In 2004 she became the first woman to command a fighter squadron. Colonel McSally flew more than 100 combat hours in an A-10 fighter jet.

Not all members of the military are human. Military working dogs are stationed around the world. Their keen noses sniff out bombs and drugs. Some dogs are trained to attack enemies. Some dogs even do parachute jumps with their handlers.

squadron—a unit of the military

Chapter 2

GETTING AROUND THE MILITARY WAY

Getting around is an adventure when you're in the military. From speedy jets and lumbering tanks to noisy helicopters and giant ships, each military vehicle has its own job to do.

The U.S. Air Force's Hurricane Hunters of the 53rd Weather **Reconnaissance** Squadron don't shelter from a hurricane. Instead, they fly their Super Hercules airplanes right into the heart of the storm to gather weather data.

reconnaissance—a mission to gather information

Nicknamed "the Warthog," the A-10 Thunderbolt II is thought to be an ugly airplane. Ugly or not, it's a mighty machine. The plane belches up to 3,900 armor-piercing shells per minute from its seven-barrel Gatling gun.

The Warthog has an armored cockpit made from titanium. This super-strong metal protects the pilot from armor-piercing shells. The cockpit's nickname is "the bathtub."

Have you ever seen a tank falling from the sky? Crews of the C-5 Galaxy have. The C-5 Galaxy is one of the biggest planes in the world. It carries tanks and drops them by parachute.

Aircraft carriers are the biggest warships in the world. The flight deck of the USS *Enterprise* is longer than three football fields. The carrier can store 60 planes with their wings folded up to save space.

Planes approach aircraft carrier runways at 200 miles (322 km) per hour. The pilot uses a hook on the plane's tail to grab a cable stretched across the flight deck. If the pilot misses and he or she can't take off again, the plane will end up in the ocean.

Aircraft carrier runways are short, so the planes need extra power for take off. Steam-powered catapults blast them into the air. A plane goes from 0 to 160 miles (257 km) per hour in three seconds.

In 1960 the nuclear submarine USS *Triton* finished the first underwater circumnavigation of Earth. It spent 60 days and 21 hours underwater.

circumnavigation—going around Earth by water

The F-16 Fighting Falcon can fly at Mach 2. That's 1,500 miles (2,414 km) per hour, or twice the speed of sound. F-16s can withstand **g-forces** up to nine Gs. That's nine times the force of gravity!

Raptors are fast, stealthy birds of prey. The F-22 Raptor is a fast, stealthy fighter aircraft. Because of its shape and onboard technology, the F-22 is almost impossible to detect by radar.

g-force—the force of gravity on a moving object

A U.S. military rocket research plane called the X-15 was the fastest, highest-flying aircraft ever. In 1963 it flew 67 miles (108 km) above Earth. Its record-breaking speed was more than 4,000 miles (6,437 km) per hour.

The CH 53-E Super Stallion is the U.S. military's biggest helicopter. It's so big it needs three engines and seven blades. It can carry 55 fully-equipped Marines or lift two Humvees off the ground.

The V-22 Osprey can hover like a helicopter and fly like a plane. Its enormous engines can be tilted up for vertical take off, or they can face forward for speedy flight.

The Stryker is an armored vehicle named after two U.S. soldiers who received the Medal of Honor. Private First Class Stuart Stryker was killed in World War II. Specialist Robert Stryker was killed in the Vietnam War (1959–1975).

British scientists think they have a way to make tanks disappear. It's called electronic **camouflage**. Pictures on the outside of the tank change to blend in with the tank's surroundings.

The Abrams tank is huge. It weighs about as much as 10 male African elephants. That could be why some people call it "the Beast."

Even the military wants to go green. The U.S. Navy is working on a plan to make fuel from pond scum, seaweed, and other types of algae. This new fuel has already been tested in a Seahawk helicopter.

camouflage—coloring or covering that makes animals, people, and objects look like their surroundings

Chapter 3

WEAPONS AND GEAR

Weapons and gear are soldiers' tools—their lives depend upon them. Rifles, grenade launchers, and unmanned vehicles are just a few of the things that make up a military's arsenal.

What's the U.S. military's top gun? It's the M16 rifle. Almost all U.S. military members learn to fire it. Military forces around the world also use M16s. More than 8 million M16s have been used since their invention.

arsenal—a place where weapons are stored

Soldiers have useful add-ons for their M16s. They can add laser pointers, night vision devices, or telescopic sights. An added-on M203 single-shot grenade launcher can blast away doors, windows, and bunkers.

Sniper weapons must be accurate over long distances. The XM2010 sniper rifle fits the bill. It has a range longer than 10 football fields.

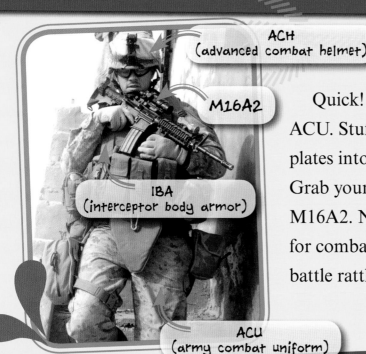

ACH
(advanced combat helmet)

M16A2

IBA
(interceptor body armor)

ACU
(army combat uniform)

Quick! Put on your ACU. Stuff your armored plates into your IBA. Grab your ACH and your M16A2. Now you're ready for combat in your "full battle rattle."

Scientists have found a way to help soldiers carry heavy loads over long distances. The HULC is a robotic exoskeleton. Wearing battery-powered titanium legs, a soldier can carry about 200 pounds (91 kilograms) of gear.

exoskeleton—a structure on the outside of a body that gives it support

A fighter jet's sharp turns and fast dives create g-forces. G-forces push blood away from a pilot's head. Pilots wear special suits so they don't pass out. The suits squeeze their lower bodies to stop blood from collecting there.

"Spin 'N' Puke" sounds like a bad fairground ride. It's the nickname of a spinning machine used to teach pilots how to deal with g-forces.

This dog doesn't bark or beg for food. But it will be a soldier's best friend. The "BigDog" Legged Squad Support System carries up to 340 pounds (154 kg) of gear.

What flies without a pilot, spies without eyes, and shoots with pinpoint accuracy? It's the remote-controlled Predator. After a mission, the Predator is taken apart and easily moved to another location.

In the future, soldiers may skitter up walls like geckos. The Z-Man program has scientists studying animals to find a way for soldiers to climb without using ropes or ladders.

We'll take the FRIES today, please. The Fast Rope Insertion/Extraction System (FRIES) is a way to get soldiers on and off the ground in seconds. The soldiers attach themselves to a rope hanging from a helicopter. Then they either slide down or climb up the rope.

The tiny Nano Air Vehicle (NAV) is the size of a sparrow. Able to hover like a hummingbird, it someday may be used to spy on enemies.

Chapter 4

MILITARY MIGHT OF THE PAST

War has existed as long as there have been people on Earth. From warriors shooting arrows to bombs dropped from planes, militaries have changed the course of history.

Dead animals as weapons? In the 1300s, militaries used catapults to launch rocks and sometimes rotting animals over castle walls. The attackers believed the rotting animals would spread disease to their enemies.

The first submarine to sink a warship was also the first submarine to be lost in battle. In 1864 the *H. L. Hunley* used the first-ever torpedo to sink an enemy ship. Then the *H. L. Hunley* sank and its crew drowned.

The 1st Minnesota Volunteer Infantry Regiment fought at the Battle of Gettysburg during the Civil War (1861–1865). When 215 of its 262 men were killed in one day, the regiment set a sad record. It was the highest casualty rate of the Civil War.

Almost 700 years ago, England and France fought the Hundred Years' War (1337–1453). English archers used bows that were as tall as the archers themselves. A good archer could shoot 10 to 12 armor-piercing arrows a minute from his longbow.

casualty—any person or group that is harmed or destroyed due to an act or event

In World War I (1914–1918), German pilots fired machine guns bolted to their planes. They fired as they flew. The guns were timed to fire between the turning propeller blades.

The United States dropped the first atomic bomb ever used in a war. It was dropped on the Japanese city of Hiroshima on August 6, 1945, during World War II. It's thought that 80,000 people died immediately. Tens of thousands more died later from **radiation** poisoning or injury.

Poison gases were first used in World War I. Soldiers were given masks that filtered the air. If no mask was available, the soldiers were told to breathe through a rag soaked with urine.

radiation—tiny particles sent out from radioactive material

The total number of deaths during World War I was 16,543,185. For each hour of the four-year war, 230 men died.

American Josephine Baker was a famous singer, actress, and dancer. And she was a spy! In World War II, she spied for France. Using invisible ink, she copied secrets onto sheets of music.

WHAT'S NEXT?

Both long ago and today, military troops and their weapons and vehicles have protected countries and the people living there. What vehicles, weapons, and gear will militaries come up with next? We don't know—it's top secret!

GLOSSARY

amphibious (am-FI-bee-uhs)—able to work on land and water

camouflage (KA-muh-flahzh)—coloring or covering that makes animals, people, and objects look like their surroundings

casualty (KAZH-oo-uhl-tee)—any person or group that is harmed or destroyed by an act or event

circumnavigation (suhr-kuhm-NAV-uh-gay-shun)—going around the Earth by water

exoskeleton (ek-soh-SKE-luh-tuhn)—a structure on the outside of a body that gives it support

g-force (JEE FORSS)—the force of gravity on a moving object

inflatable (in-FLAY-tuh-buhl)—can be filled with air

predator (PRED-uh-tur)—an animal that hunts other animals for food

radiation (ray-dee-AY-shuhn)—tiny particles sent out from radioactive material

reconnaissance (ree-KAH-nuh-suhnss)—a mission to gather information

regiment (REJ-uh-muhnt)—a large group of soldiers who fight together as a unit

squadron (SKWAHD-ruhn)—a unit of the military

unconventional warfare (uhn-kin-VEN-shun-uhl WOR-fair)—a way of fighting that is not like ordinary hand-to-hand combat

READ MORE

Fowler, Will. *The Story of Modern Weapons and Warfare.* A Journey through History. New York: Rosen Central, 2012.

Gilpin, Daniel, and Alex Pang. *Military Vehicles.* Machines Close-Up. New York: Marshall Cavendish Benchmark, 2011.

Simons, Lisa M. Bolt. *The Kids' Guide to Military Vehicles.* Kids' Guides. Mankato, Minn.: Capstone Press, 2010.

INTERNET SITES

FactHound offers a safe, fun way to find Internet sites related to this book. All of the sites on FactHound have been researched by our staff.

Here's all you do:

Visit *www.facthound.com*

Type in this code: 9781429685917

Check out projects, games and lots more at
www.capstonekids.com

INDEX